Leyla Josephine is a poet, film
from Glasgow, now based in I
Hammer and Tongue's UK Na
Championship at Royal Alber
have taken the UK by storm. *H...* ... ...
Saboteur's Best Spoken Word Show 2018, and documentation
of the show was published by Speculative Books by the
same title. *Daddy Drag* won the Autopsy Award 2019 which
celebrates artists making groundbreaking work in Scotland.
Leyla's short film *Groom* was nominated for a Scottish BAFTA
2022. Leyla's poem 'Good with our hands' was included in
Scottish Poetry Library's Best Scottish Poems of 2020. She
has been included in anthologies such as *The Edwin Morgan
Centenary Collection, Neu! Reekie! #UntitledThree* and *Choice
Words: Writers on Abortion* alongside the likes Margaret
Atwood, Audre Lorde and Gloria Steinem. She loves ABBA,
dogs, talking to her houseplants and being in the sea.

In Public / In Private

Leyla Josephine

Burning Eye

BurningEyeBooks
Never Knowingly
Mainstream

This edition published by Burning Eye Books 2022

www.burningeye.co.uk

@burningeyebooks

Burning Eye Books
15 West Hill, Portishead, BS20 6LG

ISBN 978-1-913958-35-0

Further praise for In Public / In Private:

'Beautiful and devastating. In Public / In Private is something special and we are lucky to have Leyla Josephine.'
Rachelle Atalla

'A completely stunning collection. These poems made me laugh out loud (and weep!) in public, and stayed with me for days on end in private. Leyla is a master of her craft and holds you every step of the way on this magnificent journey. Cherish it.'
Harry Baker

'In Public / In Private combines two of my favorite elements of poetry: formal play and emotional velocity. What a beautifully restless collection of psychological candor as well as of sensory and sensual vulnerability. In these pages you will encounter both wildly textured images ("It's like an advert for toothpaste but the model's got no teeth") and piercing insights into personhood ("a poem is essentially / a classy version of social media post, right?"). How startling, these poems; how uncompromisingly engaging, this poet.'
Chen Chen

'It felt somewhere between a gorgeous, warm snog and a much-needed sob on a best friend's shoulder. Beautiful, uplifting, gutting. I read it from start to finish without a breath. A triumph of a first collection.'
Hollie McNish

'Leyla sculpts poetry that bursts off the page, smouldering with sentiment, after fully inhabiting every inch of it.'
Michael Pedersen

'There is not a poet alive today who writes about the inner lives of women as well as Leyla Josephine. This breathtaking collection teases apart the difference between what is private and what is secret; what we exhibit of love, and what we keep to ourselves and our dreams.'
Jodi Picoult

Contents

I

In Public / In Private   10
This poem / The poet   11
Tell me about your vagina   12
Sleep   15
Prestwick Airport   16
Good with our hands   18
Being Scottish   19
Like   20
Spring   21
Anywhere, anything (but here)   22
Sub Club   23
Blackout   24
An interaction with a First Minister   26
A Woman Is Found Dead Mauled by Wildlife   28
Piercings   30
I first kissed a girl because the boys had asked   32
Pompeii   34

II

In Public / In Private   38
Laid   39
Wank   40
All of it   41
Times like these (2020)   42
What Do Women Want?   43
First love   44
Maman   45

Funeral   46

Bad bad girls   48

The Edge of Sanity   50

The finish line   56

Scrapbook   58

Questions I have for birds: 60

As if   62

John Cooper Clarke's rider   63

Out of reach   64

III

In Public / In Private   68

Elizabeth and her house   69

Chatroom   74

Dear John Berger   76

Potatoes   79

The girls   80

The morning after   81

Kissing in public   82

What we did in the car park of Yeats's grave   83

Our other lives   85

To the baby   87

Cherish it   88

We will never merge completely
but this is pretty close

I

In Public / In Private

Definition of *in public*:

in a place where one can be seen (by many people or one other person): there is no specification of how they are seen, if they are aware they are being seen or if there is any value/truth in what is observed.

Sentence examples: *The former actress is now rarely seen in public. They were seen kissing in public. The drunk pissed in public, a breeze on her pebbledash bum.*

Definition of *in private*:

Not in public: secret, confidential, without others seeing.

Sentence examples: *The hearings will be conducted in private. May I speak to you in private? The poet cried in private and she didn't like that no one knew; it made her question whether the crying happened at all.*

This poem / The poet

Think of this poem as a promenade / a walkway between
an amber sea and a concrete town / The poet as a tourist
on an inflatable unicorn / with sunglasses shaped as pineapples /
drinking a piña colada / waving / or maybe drowning /
drifting / ? / It's hard to tell /

Think of this poem as a nightclub / one with karaoke /
£5 cocktails / and a rattling smoke machine / The poet as the
meaty security guard / judging whether to let you in / or not /
Don't worry / she can't be too picky / the dance floor is empty /
and she'd like to take one of you home /

Okay / we're off track / Think of this poem as a lighthouse /
The poet a lighthouse keeper / Maybe you'd like to think of her
with a beard / smoking a pipe / The poet loves her job /
guiding boats to safety / It's a shame she sometimes forgets
to turn on the light / but she loves the noise the foghorn makes /
She could listen to that sound all day /

Think of this poem as a primary-school talent show / The poet
an eight-year-old girl / grinding on a chair / to 'Man! I Feel Like
a Woman!' / Don't worry if you don't know whether to laugh /
or be horrified / The girl doesn't mind / She's just happy
you're watching / She just wants to place before Avril Lavigne /

But really this poem is a window / yes / just a window / The poet
is just a poet / If you cup your hands to the glass / peep inside /
you may see the poet hasn't taken the bins out / That she didn't
get out of bed until 2pm / That she is at her desk as the last light
leaks from the room / Maybe you can see her mouth moving /
Can you make out what she's saying / ? /

Tell me about your vagina

What does it look like? Does it hang loose
or is it uptight like a mother-in-law?

Tell me about your cunt;
is that what it likes to be called? Or does it prefer flower?
If so, what kind do you think of it as?

A rose? A buttercup? A thistle?
A weed that squeezes through the cracks
looking for light? A moss perhaps?

Tell me, does it have long lips?
What secrets does it whisper at dinner tables?
Does it slurp like a child with a milkshake?

Does it groan like a patient in a ward?
Does it have teeth? Does it chatter to you
while you hoover your home?

Tell me about your pussy;
does it tremble? If so, how?
Like an earthquake? Or an airport?

An underground train?
Does it tremble like a teenager
at a Harry Styles concert?

Tell me about your slit;
is it a sponge, or a spike? A knife that slashes conversations?
Or does it only interrupt by politely raising a hand?

Tell me, does it have friends?
Ones that it welcomes in with a warm embrace?
Or is it more prone to having strangers stay uninvited?

Does it let them in? Does it give them breakfast?
Did your mother teach you that?
Do they at least pay for the damage?

Tell me about in between your legs –
the swamps of your inner thighs;
the sweat there, is it salty?

Does it taste like trifle?
Maybe banoffee? Maybe
a fine steak with gravy?

Tell me about your fanny;
where does it like to be touched?
Does it clench like buff men in gyms?

Or does it prefer to swim? Does it sing?
Where? In the shower? In the car?
What's its favourite song?

Tell me about your minge;
is it hairy? Let-it-go lairy?
Could you braid it if you wanted?

Or is it as smooth as a MacBook Pro?
Does it shed like a dog?
Do you keep the strays in a drawer?

Tell me about your vagina;
don't be embarrassed about the word.
I'll say it for you – VAGINA.

Does it weep when it bleeds? Or cackle
at the moon like the witches before it?
Is it something ancient that there is no name for?

Is it hysterical? Good. Is it trying to escape your body?
Or is it at home here? Does it like the rain?
Does it pick up stones at the beach?

What political party does it support?
Does it zip itself up when pushed into corners?
Does it have a joke it always tells?

Tell me how it acts;
does it belong to you or you to it?
What does it smell like? Does it leave a mark?

Tell me about your vagina;
are you ashamed of it?
Crossing your legs tightly in public?

Or is it celebrated in your head with champagne,
balloons and disco dancing? A hen party in your uterus?
I hope that you are proud of it.

Tell me about the crease –
the electricity that powers there.
The soft skeleton of it. The tough tissue of it.

Tell me. Tell me. Tell me. Tell me. Tell me.
Because we have all been far too quiet
and I am desperate to know.

Sleep

You're only sort of with me, in body but not in spirit. The
curtains of your eyes are sealed and keep you separated.

I am jealous of your secret worlds, the places you go without me.
You glide easily into blue pools or neon mossy lands. I am left

staring at the ceiling. Your leg jolts, scoring a goal – the crowd
goes wild. You wash windows on a skyscraper. Don't look

down. Your feet have fingers where your toes should be.
You swim surrounded by stingrays. You toss, reach for me here,

but there you're going down on someone else – an ex,
her sex smells the same as mine. You're fucking,

then suddenly you are the one being fucked. It's your future wife
with no face or temper. You try to hold her. A swollen belly.

You run, but there are coins in your shoes. You pack a rucksack
but can't find your passport. Splash,

cold water. The mirror shows your brother,
no, it's you but older. You are your mother's child,

then your mother's mum. Wading through milk,
you cum a little.

The morning slips into the room, a yawn slips into your mouth.
You come back to me softly, lock away where you've been,

and offer me a kiss. Then you start your day
like our life is the only one you live.

Prestwick Airport

*Prestwick Airport has had a strong military presence since World
War II. Most of the information is classified, but it is widely
speculated that the airport has been fundamental in refuelling
planes during various invasions of the Middle East
and transporting US prisoners of war.*

People always ask if the noise bothers me
but I have become accustomed to rattling
windows, blinking lights and a distant taste of diesel.

Outside my house, white-haired men
in body warmers stand on stepladders
watching planes through binoculars.

I survey them out the window
while I have my morning cup of tea. I am a hawk
for bald spots on these faceless men.

Their phallic camera lenses
twist in and out
like snipers ready to shoot.

I like to pretend they are paparazzi,
desperate to catch me candid
with a lover for *Hello!* or *Heat*.

I am used to budget airlines shuttling holidaymakers
to Málaga, Faros, Alicante. I imagine them clutching
matching boarding passes, giddy after 8am pints.

The other planes only come at night. They swoop in
grey and big-bellied. Bullets clink in the back
like glass bottles in a delivery truck.

They land to refuel, for soldiers to stretch their legs,
call home, tell their families they've stopped off
in the unknown.

I watch a documentary about Aleppo. A family
flees. They are the last in the city to leave.
Their sky is loaded with metal.

I sigh, switching off the TV. The rumble
drifts in and out. I sleep soundly
like it is all so far away,

like the birds have picked
out my eyes, like it has nothing
to do with me.

Good with our hands

We are welded from workers
with a sturdy way of life
metals and bolt
then planes and boats
now tech and innovation

Blue and white
men and women
who are good with their hands –
my country's pride

There are factories tattooed
across our lands
hidden in the hills
High-tech airborne radar
advanced lasers and electro-optic systems
made in Scotland but exported
worldwide

Scottish fingers fiddle to find solutions
Lanyards bounce around necks
like nooses

Staff eat their lunches
nonplussed in the cafeteria
no mutter
of Yemen
of Syria

No sign of *Nae Pasaran*

Drones, warplanes and missiles
made behind wide smiles
warm accents and cartoon thistles

My country is good with our hands

Being Scottish

It's like reaching the last hurdle in an Olympic race, only to realise you can't be arsed

It's like forgetting to press the switch when putting your phone on the charge

It's like being a bag of crisps and an elephant that lives downstairs keeps mistaking you for a seat

It's like an advert for toothpaste but the model's got no teeth

It's a soft, malleable metal that needs heat to conduct

It's being clever but knowing better than to act smart

It's shouting *It's shite being Scottish* into a mountainous abyss until a mountain looks down its nose and agrees with you

It's visiting the place you grew up, which is now a car park for a B&Q

It's a buzzard on a lamp post putting up with concrete and change

It's where wildness meets a cage

It's like being a spotty bum cheek and someone keeps whipping you with a wet towel and you keep saying that it's funny even though it hurts and you want them to stop

It's never coming to terms with what is and what always will be lost

It's where heat finds the moment, anger masks the sadness and toast melts the butter

It's being a one-pence piece dropped to the bottom of a fountain

It's reaching the last hurdle and forgetting why you're running

Like

I like to be liked / I'd like to be liked even more than I'm already liked / Like in American high school movies when the geek becomes the like hot one / She's taken her glasses off / taken her mousy hair down / and everyone all of a sudden likes her / I'd like to be liked like that /

I'd like to be an influencer / I'd get more likes / which are like little love hearts that prove you are liked / I know people don't like when you say you want to be liked / It's cooler to pretend that you don't want to be liked / but I'd be lying if I said I wasn't interested in whether people like like me or not /

Like this one time / this guy counted how many likes I said while I was talking / and he was all like do you realise how many times you just said like / ? / I was like so embarrassed / I must have really upset him / for him to humiliate me in front of the group like that / But he needs to get a life right / ? / Is there actually anything wrong with saying like / ? / Like lock me up / throw away the like key / I'm not stealing a dog or kicking your baby /

I'm not being funny but I love the word like / It gives me an extra beat to figure out what I'd like to say next / It's like a filter between my inside mind and my like outside voice / Sometimes a simple conversation can feel like a thousand thoughts hurtling towards my mouth / Like gives me a second to bat them away / I just want to make sure I say the like right thing / at the like right time / which is actually / obviously / literally / pretty likeable if you were to like ask me /

Spring

has finally sprung. The nights are getting longer
and the bluebells are in bloom.
The leaves are green.
The clocks have gone back.
The baby lambs frolic in the fields.
And I can't stop thinking about death.
Death. Death. Death.
My best friend is in labour with her first child – in spring!
How lovely! How obvious!
Death. Death. Death.
A doctor found a shadow on an X-ray in my chest – in spring!
How seasonal!
Death. Death. Death.
People are in the parks, wearing sunglasses again.
They're walking with that spring swag in their step
with their headphones in.
Have they not watched the news lately?
Do they not know a recession is coming?
The water is rising? Europe is at war? Koalas are on fire?
Someone should warn them; the flowers will soon turn to mush,
death is on the way for everyone they've ever known and loved.
There's never been so much pollution on the streets.
The lambs are born only to be knifed against metal grates.
And I was dumb to think you could be different,
that our honeymoon would never end.
I should have known you would end up in another's bed.
Someone needs to tell these fools in the park,
what I know now: beginnings are a trap!
I walk past a schmoozy restaurant,
where new couples ogle like idiots!
So smug that they've found each other,
that spring is here, that their lamb curry is delicious.

Anywhere, anything (but here)

Store me in your lighter, I'll swim laps
in the gas until you spark me into flame
to impress some girl at some bar.

Sweat me out on an inner thigh the first time it is touched
in the back seat of a Fiat 500 in a McDonald's car park
on the edge of an abandoned seaside town.

Make me a cave or a bottle or a bath.
Something that can be filled, emptied,
wet.

Sprinkle me in your knickerbocker glory,
amongst almond crumble and chocolate sauce.
Lick me off a spoon. Tell the waitress I was delicious.

Shed me as menstrual blood.
Smear me on a flushed cheek or a doughy bum
during a gymnastic sixty-nine.

Slam me as a door after an argument.
Open me with a gasp. Pick me as a scab.
Chew me up. I'll stick in your molars.

Or just take me up the dancing or out to dinner –
I need to get out of this house, this mind.
Distract me from this cage, this sad meat sack of mine.

Sub Club

The sky has caved in
and we can finally touch it.
We are abyss
dancing. Sucked into
the vacuum, side by side.
Geckos with wide eyes.
Even the light has a pulse tonight.
Stars spiral down the drains.
The bathroom has flooded
again. One-eyed gods
thud above us,
and we sacrifice
our limbs willingly.
Charging ourselves
to oblivion, swallowing
batteries. We are so high
if we died like this
it would feel right.
Taxis wait above
our submarine
on the soaked street
ready to take us
to worried parents,
but we're not finished yet.
The floor thumps
into our legs,
travels up our spines
until it feels like the music
is coming out
from our insides.
We are bleached
by strobe light.

Blackout

Q1: You wake startled in the airless tent, condensation dripping onto your face. Festival fuzz on your teeth & eyes crusted shut. Your discharged pants & muddy sundress are gossiping at your feet, but nothing has the full story. You are a blank. A male friend lies beside you fully dressed & snoring. What happened? Draw circles around three answers in each section indicating your guesses.

a)

rain	plastic ponchos	pints
bass	line, bump, line	strobe, strobe
laughter x 10	splits on a stage	sick by a bin
hands held	in the air	maybe?

b)

self-destruct button	being pressed	the sway
of crowds / of hips	stepping closer	warm breath
warm beer	taking his hand	asking for it
your fingers	his beard	you on top

c)

too much	too quickly	the ground
water sipped slowly	don't worry	she's with me
his hand	leading / forcing	the zip
of the tent	of his trousers	*no*

Q2: Your fully dressed male friend wakes up and throws you a smug smile like it was all inevitable. What happened?

a) You will never know the answer

b) But you know you don't like the question

c) Not one bit

An interaction with a First Minister

for the nine women who cannot be named

I

His assistant, drenched in Chanel,
herded us like sheep.
Her eyes scanned us
up and down
as if we were thieves.

Everyone showered him with ego
over finger sandwiches at the grand table.
His smile diamanté wet and glass –
a salesman with nothing to sell
but himself.

The show started –
we gaped at the pantomime
personalities plated.

His glitter was faceted
and we closed our eyes
dazzled by it.

We were an obedient audience.
We sensed when to clap,
gasp, laugh,
shake our heads,
when to shut our mouths.

I left feeling dirty and opaque.
I had undone myself in there.
Spellbound by fools' gold,
the rush of it all.

II

The papers repeat the word *alleged*
the way a drum keeps a rhythm.
It sets the tone for the rest of the read,
but the graphics still manage to push through –

working late, pencil skirts
pushed around waists, his clammy
hands with blotched skin,
her eyes closed.

She *alleges* he *hunted* her –
a heavy word for a piece of meat
that is laid flat and plays dead,
but we all know exactly what she means.

III

He is a magician and he promised us freedom.
We are white bunnies with scarlet eyes
longing to be released from black hats
and we excuse him, we are desperate.

We women know what it's like
to be presented to a crowd
like we are playing a part,
presented as whole
when we have just been cut in half.

A Woman Is Found Dead Mauled by Wildlife

The article doesn't specify what creature picked at her.
The village whispers: fox, badger, maggot,
deer, rabbit, crow? My money is on crow.
But it is all speculation. What do we know?

A Woman Is Found Dead Mauled by Wildlife
Four days before Christmas. Her car broke down.
She phoned for help. They were on their way, but
she didn't wait. She strayed off into nearby fields.

A Woman Is Found Dead Mauled by Wildlife
After her car broke down. She walked away
from the green glow of the garage. Away from
the throb of the motorway into unlit fields.

A Woman Is Found Dead Mauled by Wildlife
One mile away from her car. A Citroën. Four days
before Christmas. She phoned for help. She did not
wait. She wandered into the wilderness.

A Woman Is Found Dead Mauled by Wildlife
The village whispers wildness. One mile from the safe
garage. Strayed into the throb of unlit fields. Towards
the crows, she walked.

A Woman Is Found Dead Mauled by Wildlife
Pecked on by maggots, foxes, rabbits. She strayed
away from paper routines. The green glow. Into whispers
she wandered. One mile from her broken-down car.

A Woman Is Found Dead Mauled by Wildlife
Strayed away from help. The garage. This metal world.
The village. The article doesn't specify what colour
of Citroën. The fields whisper; what do you wish you knew?

A Woman Is Found Dead Mauled by Wildlife
Was she herself not a wild life? The article doesn't specify.
Did she stray from time spent bent-necked? Her Citroën?
Christmas? Was it a choice to walk into wilderness?

A Woman Is Found Dead Mauled by Wildlife
Did she lie herself down in unlit fields, one mile from help,
in the churned-up earth? The article doesn't specify,
but we, the village, wonder.

Piercings

I

On the pleather fold-out, the inked man in latex gloves
smeared cold gel on my plummy stomach.

I picked a baby blue gem, like Xtina, like the sky
in California, like the eye colour I miserably wanted.

I tried to think of anything but the stiff bar
being inserted through me

but my mum had worried herself into my head.
My puppy rolls wept.

For days I watched it rise and fall,
felt sick, couldn't take it anymore.

Tugged it clean out.
Took a week off school.

II

Orla wanted her tongue done. We hitchhiked to a town
where we were unknown. Our lift grinned, solid in his seat.

I watched a Sharpie dot the dank spot. A simple click.
It was done. She'd made her mark.

We toasted to each other with Fat Frogs in the square.
Our mouths sweetshop green. Her tongue dumpy and sore.

When drunk enough, we bounced to the Unders.
Our pleated skirts blew up in the smoke machine wind.

In dingy corners, tracksuit boys with gelled hair tongued
glittered girls, their hands crept up thighs into wet lilac thongs.

The bus home was a snake pit. We swirled into each other
as the night sucked the light from the corners.

My friend's tongue winked at me like a serpent's eye
flashing its way through the darkness.

Back home, she spoke with her mouth closed
but her mum heard the lisp.

She stuck her hand deep into Orla's throat
and Orla opened herself up willingly.

It was the closest thing to sex I'd ever seen.

III

The first lip that touched my clit was pierced.
I was pressed to the wall of the Protestant church by the pier.

I didn't know what was metal or what was the cold night
or what a clit was.

For weeks, I was convinced I was pregnant, couldn't shake
the feeling of something foreign I needed to expel.

Mum shot me side glances,
smelling the metal, sensing the change.

I first kissed a girl because the boys had asked

they asked nicely so i chewed on her like bubblegum

her bubble bath lavender scent / my hair / her lip gloss

her lip gloss / my wetness

my wetness must have been because the boys watched

the boys watched so i got wet / i told myself

i told myself forget about this first time

*

the first time i touched a girl between her legs i couldn't help it

couldn't help reaching for her / a way to get out

out of my own body

my own body not mine yet

yet managed to use it / to touch her / in my childhood bedroom

our shared childhood / a sleepover / a cliché

clichéd ourselves girls / we cut her hair

her red hair / hung around / longer than she did

she did seem to like it / the haircut / the secret

the secret was kept

but i kept finding red strands

strands stuck in floorboards / magazines / between bedsheets between toes / reminding me what i had done

    done what i said i wouldn't / and worse / i liked it

liked it / but denied it / for a decade

*

    a decade later it was different with you

you different you / no one watched

    no one there but us / except a cat on a car bonnet

the bonnet reflected orange lights / the full moon

    a full moon in libra / my old self eclipsed

eclipsed behind you / different you / i was so into you

    into your mustard coat i cried

i cried because i was saying goodbye to questions

    questions that i had never liked

i had never liked that part of me / but it was painful

    yes / it was painful just the same

Pompeii

I liked having her in my bed
spilling sinked in and sticky
Folded into each other
like flatpack furniture
I held on to her
a little bit longer
than I should have

She was softer than I expected
kind right through to her edges
Still she was fiery
I tricked her
accidentally
She stumbled
invested suddenly
tiptoeing hands
politely
going
down
slowly
careful
not to
rush me
I'm so sorry

We would wake in the night
all hot and twisted
I'd call her after clubs
tell her that I'd missed it
She would fire over
hold me like a flame
tears after I came

I treated her
like men
had treated me

I never knew how else
to look at a woman

Eventually I burnt her out
feeling scorched
scorn and torn
too much trouble
smoke
I am a blaze
amazed
she couldn't see
how I masked
in her ash

I wish I had told her
everything
I wish she had asked

II

In Public / In Private

pri open the jar, you may need a dish towel to get a good grip,
peer in to see what fruits are inside. stick your finger in the goo.
no scentless supermarket strawberries here. these fruits are
different to the red flavour of a car's air freshener. these are not
the synthetic additives that you're used to.

vate is the latin poet, withdrawn and stressed, chewing pens.
the genii are in the walls flapping and whispering guidance
but the poet's ears are full of wax, ego and worry that his
parents will disapprove.

pub is where the people gather. the champion is the one who
buys two packets of crisps without being asked, splits them
open, revealing the metallic inside, and says *help yourself.*

lic the spoon. the tongue leaves the body, as a snail leaves the shell.
a spectacle for everyone to see. the white fur on your tongue
reveals the toxins that multiply inside your liver, the desires
you gave in to, the ones you could not resist.

Laid

If I had been
just a little bit drunker this evening
I would have taken you home
laid you down like a mountain
covered you in moss and pine
left footprints on your skin
spun rainstorms in your mouth
I would have taken myself
to bathe in the waters
of your south

Wank

uneven boobies bruiser inked forearms salmon dicks bounding upstr
bouncing bums eating cycling shorts glistening armpits knobbly knees
wobbly thighs streaky tan like bacon ripped off the skin i'm into in bet
the toes the clink of teeth salty white seep hips bending in impossible
tongues and tongues and tongues and tongues and pillows with bite m
and socks kept on how glad i am i walked shame to the door gave it its
fare sent it back to wherever it came from pubes fluttering like eyelas
human sap smeared on tummies jelly slurped off hands like honey
in my head i'm free to experiment god is only raging because
he can't stop it sure it's nice to be pressed into
lovers but better yet to be let loose
inside my head a dip into yours
truly this black hole
swallowing stars
i am wide open
a tunnel
a mouth
a lake
a hole
a dig
into
myself
find
the light
the uvula
the treasure
the heaven
the bottom
i won't stop
i'm almost
there

All of it

I like how you touch me
while you're driving
eyes rolling
off the
                road
ahead of us
I'm slipping
dripping sipping
on you
burying myself
in your
nape
            escape
push pull
back
an elastic attack
no need to fake it
you're the best at it
side of the road
spit on me
clip it for me
lick its spine baby
clapping our knees
feeling me
tangle and tease
your breath
earthy breeze
please
just a little bit at first
then all of it
I want
all
of
it

Times like these (2020)

Time is
        stuck
like a printer jammed with paper
like a jumper's thread on a nail
like chewing gum stuck on a shoe
watery dog shit on a carpet

We are flies
lolling in caramel
smothered by our wants
gasping for breath
wings peeling off our spines
the back of our throats
sickly sweet
syrup-strangled
– what a way to go –
overindulged and
dead!

The wind changed
and we're
stuck
        here
our faces contorted
in gob smack
like frozen
woolly mammoths
caught by the ice

Like the horizon is
burning
– and rightly so –
and our hands are
gripping the past
and we are all
too stubborn
to let go

What Do Women Want?

after Kim Addonizio

I want to wear a long red silk dress with nothing underneath /
I want a man in some seedy city to slip me an envelope / I want to
lick the salt off a margarita and make my way to an elevator /
I want eyes to follow me and mouths to swallow me / I want to be
wrong for the job and get it anyway / I want heels on cobbles and
fucking in taxis / I want applause / The butler with his champagne
on ice / I want praise for what I say / not what I do / I want the dawn
and the zombies / My blood on his shirt / I want the drugs and
I want them for free / The jewelled shoes and quilted bag / I want
the girls with their collarbones freckled from the sun / I want the men
Rolex-wristed / with their big hands on me / I want you on your knees /
begging for more / I want to get away with it all / by the skin
of my goddamn teeth /

First love

He liked choking me while we fucked
I liked making him happy so I didn't mind

One time in the deep heat of July he stuck
his dick so far down my throat

I threw up in my mouth and I drank it down
so he wouldn't think badly of me

He kept saying that there was a weird smell
I kept saying I didn't smell a thing

I went to the bathroom downed a whole bottle
of mouthwash I didn't spill a drop

I loved him so much that if he asked nicely
I would have let him kill me

I would still let him kill me if it meant
he would put his hands on me one last time

Maman

I stared up into the belly of a giant metal spider
Her eight legs cast in thick ribbed bronze

Thirty-two marble eggs in her nest
hanging at a copper abdomen

Spiders spin silk sacs to protect their children
I was pregnant by the autumn

In hospital with my legs parted
a pain weaved through my body like spit

I told my mum about the procedure
She wept like I had killed something inside her

In October spiders leave their neuks to mate
In bed one dragged herself across my body

I a landscape her a pilgrim Her animal need
– a starless calling deep within

Spiderlings eat their mother when she is close to death
I lodged copper in my cervix to stop life latching on again

Funeral

My stilettos sink into the grass
My new coat has fur around the collar
I chose my outfit to align with gold-digger
rather than grieving-daughter

I am asked to throw dirt
on a box that supposedly
has my dad in it
Hundreds of eyes are watching me
wondering why I am not crying

What will I do with the dirt on my hand?
Rub it on my aunty's black dress
as she grips me?
Maybe I should lap it clean?
Or force my fist into my mouth?
Give the crowd something to talk about
Maybe I should clamber into the grave
like a dramatic soap actress
or a child woken from a nightmare

I could curl into him
his body now a question
mark his body now yellow
amongst soil mites
and seedlings
his body now stacked
on top of my cousin
my uncle
their suicides

If I start crying
I might never stop
So I laugh instead

My mouth is full of bones breaking
It cracks the frosty morning in half
My audience are horrified
As they should be

We make our way
back to the car
I take my shoes off
my tights sodden
with dew
The hearse driver
in his black hat yawns
like he's seen it all before
but I consider it my best
performance to date

Bad bad girls

want it rough
swallowed whole
looked through
preparing
best they can
like frosted
perspex
men
lick their lips
suck their teeth
their hands on
bad bad girls
necks like rope
burn
bad bad girls
flicked at the chin
the men rasp
just give in
just give in
bad bad girls
want it
so bad
they're dying
for it
with doughy eyes
uh uh uh
bad bad girls
face the bare wall
feathers
plucked
one by one
to be
glazed
gobbled
consumed
spat out

bad bad girls
tell men
they want it
and maybe they do
bad bad girls
are bad bad sluts
for asking for it
rough then
harder
and
harder
to feel something
shatter
because honey
you barely
touch
the edges

The Edge of Sanity

Dialogue between grieving woman and chorus.

WOMAN:
Firstly, some advice
I have been given:

                                        CHORUS:
                                  You have to make
                          a companion out of death.
                             You must make yourself
                                  your own best friend.
                          Lower your expectations.

WOMAN:
That one has always worked best.
One thing I know is that my family
are good at funerals.
We line the bodies up on the planks
and count how many have drowned...
Too many.

                                        CHORUS:
                     Have you drowned yourself lately?
                             You had swimming lessons
                     at the leisure centre, did you not?
                           Your father, he drowned, right?
                        A bad captain *and* a pervert?!

WOMAN:
My dad used to lie me on the bathroom floor
and steam up the room on nights
I was struggling to breathe, and wrapping
myself around the toilet to cool my forehead
has never failed. I would do the same
at parties or clubs after I'd thrown up.
I met a ghost in there once
and he told me to slow
                          down.

I was so freaked out
I never told anyone
and had a tequila instead.

CHORUS:
Your da said –
if you can't get it down ye,
get it up ye!

WOMAN:
And that one has also worked best.

I read *Grief Is the Thing with Feathers*.

CHORUS:
The thing has wings!
It's the fly on your ceiling!
The crow! The pigeon!
Or face-down on the carpet!

WOMAN:
And the carpet never talked back,
not once. But one time at a party,
a red wall became hollow.
I entered and found myself
at the base of a tree and realised—

CHORUS:
Let us guess!
Let us guess!
Everything is *connected*

WOMAN:
I saw primary school and roots
and veins and I scrabbled back out
and woke to see a girl I didn't like
tripping harder than me
and I felt sympathy for her.

CHORUS:
She was no doubt
a mirror.

WOMAN:
All the men that I have dated
have been similar to my father.

CHORUS:
Freud called it!
You have to live it!

WOMAN:
I always choose men that are broken.
Just a wee bit more broken than me.

CHORUS:
They are perfect
because you get to pretend
that you are nailing it.

WOMAN:
I get so distracted by boys
and how they glisten and never listen.
Their minds are purple to me.
The last one I went for was a dentist,
he came in his hand in the end—

CHORUS:
A modern romantic!

WOMAN:
He sat at the opposite side of the room
refusing to look at me. I called a taxi.
In the back seat, I tapped my ruby heels,
disappointed he had failed to fuck
the feelings from me.

CHORUS:
Well, at least
you looked good
from behind.

WOMAN:
My mind sometimes runs

away

from me.
I wish it would run to
a quiet place,
a garden space maybe,
or a pond or a bog or a cliff
but it just stands at the edge
of this?

CHORUS:
Simply impossible, isn't it?

WOMAN:
How long has it been?

CHORUS:
It was two weeks,
then four years,
now eight.

WOMAN:
It comes back in spirals to haunt me.
At least these pricks want me.

CHORUS:
Prick,
prick,
drip drip,
we've found
ourselves back
at the family
epicentre quick.

WOMAN:
Maybe grief is that feeling
you get alone in your bedroom.
When you could swear
there is someone behind you –
a presence you just can't shake.

CHORUS:
How does it feel to have ghosts
watch you masturbate?

WOMAN:
I've always felt alone,
a lonely child.

CHORUS:
Curse of the only child.

WOMAN:
Grabby for attention.

CHORUS:
Doesn't it feel good to finally be able
to give your shitty behaviour
an excuse, a reason?

WOMAN:
I wish I could be subtle,
closed, smaller.

CHORUS:
Have you ever considered
it could be you who is similar
to your father?!

WOMAN:
Grief is: a woman, sitting at a kitchen table, smoking cigarettes,
quietly crying. It is white pain in my jaw, clamping down on
myself in my sleep, in case my soul escapes or a spirit tries to
steal my teeth. It is a crowd of people; I am in the middle making
eye contact with everyone to see which one can destroy me the best.
It is going into a room and forgetting the point. It is rust and
waves, square eyes from too many screens and duvets made of
porridge. It is a dead horse on a motorway, a dead dad floating in
a harbour. It is wearing the same hoody every day for a month.
It is rotten orange juice in the fridge and having someone inside
me that makes me feel alive and dead and like sand
and like time
is running out
while he is
running
down
my
leg.

                                     CHORUS:
                                     This is ego!
                Think of all who have it worse.

WOMAN:
It is grief and I don't want it!

                                     CHORUS:
                     Hah. Why lie to yourself?
                You have always been like this.

WOMAN:
How do I make a mark
when I don't know how to use a pen
and can't find a piece of blank paper?
When my throat is filled with dampness,
my forehead's pressed against the toilet,
and I need everyone to drop everything
and please just come to the rescue and
show me how I am meant to do this.

The finish line

Nelly isn't wearing her own glasses. Still better
than last week when she wasn't wearing her own teeth.

Nelly's skin hangs onto her skeleton
like wet clothes just out the wash,

her collarbone a thin plastic
the rest of her body is draped on.

She has been faced to the nineties telly glaikit;
white rust lines her downturned mouth.

Coverage of the London Marathon fizzes
through the crusty quiet.

My nose burns – custard, shit, beef and bleach.
A hospital cocktail

Another patient in her chair
covered in crumbs calls us cunts.

Nelly twists at her wedding ring.
Slips her slippers on and off.

Since my last visit all the art has been taken down,
staff sick of prising frames from the residents' grip.

Pictures now are painted straight onto the walls:
a field of poppies, a bowl of peaches, a kitten in a basket

stares lifelessly at me. I want to avoid eye contact
with everything, so my eyes find the TV.

Spectators spectate the spectacle,
take photos on their phones.

A presenter shouts energetically into a mic.
Everyone is all high-fives, sore limbs, sweaty hugs.

Runners reach the finish line,
jump and punch the air.

They seem to be really glad
that it's finally all over.

Scrapbook

The spine creaks open like a door to an attic
I am greeted with whiffs of wet paper
and a dried insect or two

Black-and-white photos of old friends, young
smile out at me begging for recognition
but I am a blank

The corners of the pages are receding
squinting needed to read the backs of postcards
signed *Jane* or *Sue* or *Your Darling x*

A sketch of a trawler, a bottle cap, an invitation
to a Playboy party, pictures from the Navy –
California, Vancouver, Osaka

I visited there too, Dad, me too!

I pull it out from time to time
an archaeologist digging for clues
analysing the artefacts

I'm left with nothing but soot on my fingertips
regret for the questions I did not ask
the time I spent in my room

When I die (hopefully like a rockstar)
and my overwhelmed children
are clearing out my stuff

they will ask
is this treasure
or is this trash?

I guess the scrapbook
will be rubbish by then
a man they never knew

and it will be easier
to let that life slip away
to wherever the forgotten go

Questions I have for birds:

Where do you go at night?
How do you hear without any ears?
Does it hurt when you lose a feather?
Are you friends with one another?

You know the worms you strangle out of the earth
like screaming red newborns?
Do you chew? Or gobble them whole?
I've never seen a glint of a tooth, so I guess that's how it works.

Is it like swallowing a piece of spaghetti? Is it like sucking
your tongue to the spine? Could you confirm?
Can you feel them squirm in your belly
like eels, until the acid melts them to mush?

I see you on windy days, flying harder and for longer;
is there more joy in that kind of weather?
Gusty and unpredictable. Do you feel invincible?
I see how you dip and glide,

a moment of clarity, a break
from the monotony of a daily bird routine.
What does that feel like? If you had time
to explain, I'd love to know.

Is it like a child slapping their palms down on the ocean top?
Or lesbians kissing hard on the street? How a violin string feels
when it is plucked? Does it make you vibrate? Like an old man
shouting *checkmate* in a park with a board on a bench?

Pardon the pun, but is it like a duck to water?
Is it like coming up on a dance floor?
The first taste of ice cream off a mum's pinky?
What is a human's version of flying when it's windy?

Does it feel like your purpose?
Do you get lost in it?
Birds, tell me what I can do
to have those moments always:

on the wind, on the surf,
on the nose, on the breeze.
The clarity. The coming together.
That's what life is for, maybe?

Sorry, I brought it back to myself again.
Now, do say, how do you stand on such small feet?
Do you have a favourite seed?
How do you know what song to sing?

As if

Take me to the ocean on your back.
Show me the islands being eaten
by the horizon. Tell me their names
in a language I no longer know.
Let's put aside the hard truth –
you are leaving and soon. Wait
with me on the cliff, by the holy
patch of cottongrass dancing. Wait
with me until the sky stains
the water flamingo pink. Wait
with me until we spot orcas
out by the wind farm. Painting themselves
through the sea in figures of eight. Let's squint
and point and shout *there, just there!*
As if we have never seen anything so fucking beautiful.
As if their beauty would make this last.
As if nothing will ever change.

John Cooper Clarke's rider

10 bottles of water
A box of Yorkshire Tea
A pint of semi-skimmed milk
A score of heroin not taken
A family pack of Mini Rolls
Portrait of a Lady aftershave
(The smell of it in the corridor,
on my clothes after a hug)
A multipack of McCoy's crisps
A pair of jet black Ray-Bans
One pack of Lucky Strike
Nostalgia
2 chicken sandwiches
The sickness that comes from writing
The loneliness of living twice
Black hair dye
A bottle of gin
A single lemon
Ice
&
Wings

Out of reach

I have an urge to reach out and grab
the stranger's hand at the next table.
Maybe it's the indie playlist that's playing in this café
or how the trees from the park cut the light that skims the table
or that I am hungover and I miss you.

I have an urge to fill my house with plants
so I am not the only breathing thing.
I have an urge to shave my head
so more people ask me why I have a shaved head.
I have an urge to become TikTok famous –
I write a poem instead
because a poem is essentially
a classy version of a social media post, right?

Reader, are you here with me?
Can you give me a sign?
Does a poem have a skin you can peel?
Are we dancing together inside it?
If you could grab my hand, would you?

Or are we always just out of reach?
A page-thin distance, a world away?
The poem always hovering at the doorway of itself,
a modified architecture of reality, carefully edited,
a substandard shadow of what I'm trying to show you?

I'm asking because the way
this afternoon light hits
the table is making me
so lonely.

The way it pirouettes
just to break itself into pieces
makes me think
that maybe the light
is lonely too.

So I'll keep trying.
Reader, I'll go on.

III

In Public

i am wide hands / roar and stomp / i am all arms and lips /
teeth and war / i am showtime / shouting / unforgiving and
mostly drunk / i am hard shell and shots / i am muddy trainers
and swish of hair / i am all cross and red / flirty and hot / i am
filling space and chewing gum / smoking and
hailing taxis / last orders and interrupting / i am piggybacks
and limbo dancing / i am all force and sure / rain and storm

/ In Private

i am windows open and taps turning off / i am embarrassed
and soft / tired and folded / i am legs curled and face washed /
warm tea and planes passing overhead / i am gravel
and dirt / plant and stone / slug and snail / i am spider / i am
thought and wishes / worry and witch / i am room corners and
sitting on the floor / i am drying dishes and the radio
is filling my home

Elizabeth and her house

This is a cautionary tale
about a woman named Elizabeth
who naively downloaded
an app for mindfulness.

Chanting monks and hypnotic bells
tuned her to the moon.
She claimed she reached enlightenment
staring at her reflection in a teaspoon.

She'd never properly looked around
to witness the magic in every day;
she'd been distracted by this and that.
She made a pact to live in a new way.

She had wasted so much time
worrying her little head.
She made a promise to be grateful
for everything from now until death.

She was in love with the small things.
She didn't need much else.
She could make herself happy
by simply being present in the house.

Elizabeth started spending
more and more time alone;
she considered herself flourishing
now she was riding solo.

She rediscovered herself bit by bit
as if she was an island.
She'd wasted too much time
searching for others on the horizon.

It became a love affair, this new intimacy
with herself and the house.
She quit her job, sold the car
and completely stopped going out.

She threw away her phone.
She closed the blinds.
She got shopping delivered
until her card eventually declined.

She snubbed her friends, patched
the neighbours, ignored her mum;
they didn't understand or accept
the new person she'd become.

There was no point in cleaning,
no longer did things need washed.
Personal hygiene was a waste of time
and indefinitely paused.

She drank tea from prosecco flutes,
scranned porridge from a pot,
put ketchup in an ashtray,
ate soup with a fork.

She played chess with the spiders,
badminton with the moths.
She took to wandering naked
or dressed in only a tablecloth.

She would striptease at her wardrobe
like it had a fist full of fivers.
She sang and pleasured herself,
cursing her past lovers.

Elizabeth was enjoying her environment
a little too much.
She would get a fanny-flutter
at every item she used or touched.

She would lick her plate
for longer than she should,
brush her breasts
along the floor's hardwood.

With no one around she indulged
in her fantasies;
she played footsy with the toaster,
fingered statues on the mantelpiece.

She would stroke the iron
in between her thighs,
ride her chaise longue
like it needed the exercise.

She sucked on every spine
on every book;
lingering on her belongings
felt deliciously good.

She French-kissed
every handbag and every shoe.
She made love to the electrics
and lightbulbs blew.

She fucked every piece of cutlery
from the drawer,
then moved on to the hoover
until she was sore.

She swallowed and spat
the filling from her couch.
By the end, she had tasted and banged
every surface in her house.

Her screams were heard
two doors down at number six,
but they had their own reasons
to keep their heads down and stay out of it.

She did to things what lovers had done to her.
They had always been a bit rough.
But Elizabeth wasn't satisfied,
objectifying her objects wasn't enough.

The mirror started looking at her funny,
the stairs laughed behind her back,
the radiators gossiped,
she got weird vibes off the shoe rack.

Grinding with a cheese grater,
she cut herself loose.
The bed wouldn't let her out,
even when she slept the whole night through.

She couldn't remember
what she was trying to prove.
She started to stiffen,
unable to move.

It was as if she was wet concrete
trickling into the cracks,
becoming harder and harder
with every day that passed.

She gazed from her bed to the street,
somewhere she used to exist.
Was this what she had wanted?
Was this what she had wished?

She was as thin as the draught
sweeping along the floor.
She started feeling numb;
Elizabeth was done for.

She became slates, mortar, brick,
made of solid thoughtlessness.
She was the walls and the walls
were her fortress.

On her last day, she smelt her sheets
and counted her blessings.
She was unsure what else to do
with her final seconds.

A car went by and lit up
her pale, gaunt face,
and she just slipped off
into some inanimate place.

Chatroom

UKBD45:   Hey :)

Frda33:   hi :) howz you?

UKBD45:   gd u?

Frda33:   yea gd gd

UKBD45:   R u alone? ;)

Frda33:   yea :)

UKBD45:   What u wearin?

Frda33:   black stockins n Lacy pants. Nuthin else...

UKBD45:   fuck !!

UKBD45:   Im hard thinkin abot u

UKBD45:   R U a slut?

Frda33:   4 u yea i am. Wht would u do 2 me if we wer 2gether?

UKBD45:   Pull ur panties to the side so i cud feel how wet u r :P

Frda33:   Im touchin myself

UKBD45:   i miss ma mum

Frda33:   wht?

UKBD45:   Soz I dnno y i said tht

Frda33:   thats ok

UKBD45:   ur kind?

Frda33:   wht wer u expectin?

UKBD45:   i dnno

Frda33:   u cnt fuck a rock?

UKBD45:   na but u can hold it

Frda33:   i like how a stone feels in my palm whn the
            sun has been on it all day

UKBD45:   Sumtimes I feel like a brick wall watchin wild
            flowerz

Frda33:   cover me like the sun heats ah stone

UKBD45:   Im close

Frda33:   Im here

UKBD45:   Im done

Frda33:   nite. xo

UKBD45:   wait

Frda33 is no longer available.

Dear John Berger

My name is Leyla and I'd like to invite you to my celebrity (dead or alive) dinner party. I'm a big fan of your work – especially your book/BBC documentary *Ways of Seeing*.

John, I wanted to ask you a question: if no one is looking at me, do I still exist? My boyfriend has moved out and I'm not sure anymore. I run a bath but when I get in the water doesn't ripple. Now he's gone, I only answer to me – but I'm going straight to voicemail. John, you said *Whilst [a woman] ... is walking across a room or whilst she is weeping at the death of her father, she can scarcely avoid envisaging herself walking or weeping*. John, how did you know I wept over my father's death? How did you know I have walked across many rooms? Once IRL and then again in my head as stuffy critic. John, how did you get so smart? You said *[A woman] ... is almost continually accompanied by her own image of herself*, so why do I still feel so lonely? I was thinking about filling my house with mirrors so I don't feel alone, but I only like my reflection from 3.5 angles.

So, I've been leaving the house to seen by other people. I go to coffee shop chains – they are the perfect place to pretend to be a real person. I go through the motions: order a chai latte, chip and PIN, pat the collie under the table, type on my laptop like it means something. Little girls are the first to notice me, John. In fact, one is staring at me right now. Her eyes are telescopes searching for a future self. I want to tell her: Stop! It's a trap! I want to tell her: don't look at me, I don't know how to be a woman! I want to whisper to her: The hairier I am, the sexier I feel! But I don't, I just stare back – it's good practice.

When I was small my dad would make me do little tricks for his work mates in the pub. I learnt that eyes were valuable, that oily hands would clap if I twirled fast enough. John, I could make grown men light up like puggy machines. I don't remember the Shania Twain incident at the primary school *Stars in Your Eyes* talent show. But I know I was on brand. I know I wore a leopard-print leotard and a top hat. I know afterwards I told everyone that I had *caught the fame bug*. The next day the teacher announced to the class I was a *show off*. Is there anything worse than someone calling you a show off? It makes me want to crawl into my own stomach and die there. Maybe that's what I should tell the little girls: being a good woman means showing off, but never so much that someone might notice.

John, I hate to admit it, but I love being seen. It comforts me to know that I am in the background of lots of strangers' photographs. I like fucking musicians and then pretending their songs are about me. I am only helpful to other writers so I can get into the acknowledgment sections of their books. I lost a diary and a psychic told me a small man with a small name took it. I don't remember what was in the diary, but I know it wasn't meant for the small man with the small name, and now he knows me intimately in a way no one else does. It used to keep me up at night, this thought, but now it is camomile.

John, if a woman cums alone, does a tree fall in a forest? John, the house is so empty, I can hear the glass in the windows breathe. John, If a man broke in and held a hammer to my head I might kiss him. John, what do you do to make your hair so soft? I wish I could touch it. I'm sure your eye contact would be second to none. I'm sure your eyes would linger respectfully on my braless tits over the pita breads. I bet you drink an old fashioned, don't you John? If you say yes, I'll get the bitters in. Our dinner party could be so special. If our legs touch under the table, I bet I will ripple.

John, I wonder how he remembers me. I wonder if he remembers the way his pupils would open up like rocket ships. John, maybe you could paint me naked – no, nude.

I could send it to him. Maybe he would hang it on his wall and let my acrylic eyes meet his distant ones. John, embalm me. Paint me like one of your French girls. Paint me holding a mirror. Maybe he will name it *Vanity* – let him.
We'll call it – *A Woman's Corner*.

John, please come over, I'd like to scoop your eyes out with a fork. I'd like to keep them by my bed in a small velvet box. I'd like to take them out from time to time – watch you watch me. I didn't think you'd mind, since you're dead and everything.

Maybe this is something we could discuss at dinner.

John, would you mind stoping off at Iceland on your way and picking up a Vienetta?

Leyla

Potatoes

My mum calls me from her new house
I wish you could see the sunset here

I assure her I am looking at the same sky
only on another cut of rock

She breaks the news – *my garden's soil
is infertile* – there's too much salt

from the Atlantic sea. She's gutted
she can't grow her yearly potatoes

This summer is the first we are countries apart
and the first I have a garden. I plant potatoes

In boiling nights I dream of a foetus
I dig her up from the turf. Brushing dirt

gently from her face. I wake as empty
as a shell, the dream rooted into my days

I carry her like a phantom limb. A plump hand on my neck
a mouth on my breast, a tiny head on my shoulder

What I should have said is this: *Mum, I want to trace
your C-section scar with my mouth*

I want to taste the dark grove I grew from
My child would have been eight this year

Mum taught me that if potatoes are brought to the surface
too early they can be poisonous

I am unsure if the timing is right, but I risk it
I crunch into a purple spud straight from the umber earth

Soil on my lips. Starch on my tongue. A spider spits
a home from itself. The sun births a bloody sky

*Mum, I don't have the words to explain my love for living things
the thrill to taste something I have grown all by myself*

The girls

i've got the girls / forever / they've been with me / staggering
down streets / laughing / dancing / on tables / girls / with our
tales that we keep / for takeaway meals / girls / hold your
hand / make you tea / come to bed with me girl / seas separate
us sometimes / but somehow we come home / to melt / into each
other / always / the girls / mac counter warriors / belts of lipstick
weapons / contouring is witchcraft / fuck him / fuck that / taking
our bodies back / bring the girls out of the dark / into highlighter
herstory / the girls / just try to call us / hysterical girls / fire in our
cheeks girls / keys between our knuckles girls / the betrayed again
girls / when we are alone / you underestimate us / but together
we take up the pavement / cemented / and you feel threatened /
my girls / our love stories are the greatest never told / we are the
bold girls / the too much girls / we laugh as loud as our mothers /
feel the moon in our waters / we don't chew when we eat / forget
to breathe when we speak / we are the don't interrupt us girls /
the angry girls / the silenced girls / the dangerous girls /
the we're coming for you / girls /

The morning after

In your flat, we are face-down on the carpet. We are spilt drinks
seeping towards each other. We are hungover.

Your boyfriend's banjo slumps against the wall. A cowboy
reminding us of our slurred singing into dawn's first scatterings.

The apogee of the night came and went, we continued taking
no notice. Like antlers carved from skin, our arms led us dancing,

our feet following; our men were merely there out of a traditional
obligation. We were flammable and they were rightly cautious.

Babbling, cackling, we tapped Marlboro Golds into an ashtray –
a woman's bum, pink as prawns. I bought her as a joke

but she stuck around. Her cavernous ass fills with ash from our twos.
She is as much part of our bevy as we are. She knows it all –

our red hands, our loose lips. But you are the main event,
my dazzling friend – oh, the trouble we get in.

The day is already half-eaten, much like our breakfast.
Buttered rolls and tatty scones are already hardening in us.

Cold tea stains the mugs; we also grow a milky skin.
We are sickly and definitely too old for this.

But I could lie here forever skimming the night before for stories
to regorge, with our guttural laughs – *our let's gut them all* laughs.

You're the arson to my arse. You set my world alight,
my firework friend.

Kissing in public

We winch like old Hollywood starlets and restaurant patrons try
not to watch us – but they can't help it, and I can't blame them;
this is an unmissable kiss. I'm not sure where you start and I sto
We are endless. It's like I have just chased you through an airpo
and have convinced you to stay. Or like there has been a zombie
infection in our city, the cure is lodged somewhere in your throa
and I must dislodge it before the hour is out. We're making face
love in this red velvet booth. Customers peek over sticky menus
The waiter pretends to polish cutlery. We ignore them; in this scrip
it's just you and me, baby! We kiss like there has been a nuclear
explosion, and we both survived the initial blast, but the only
clean air left is in our lungs, and we must kiss until the dust
settles and the radiation has gone. I kiss you like I am a cowboy
in the wild, wild west and you are my faithful, faithful horse.
The only one who understands my quiet disposition, why I wea
my trousers so high, my manly frustrations. I kiss you like I hav
just dragged you from the ocean and you need mouth to mouth,
and I insist in performing CPR even though I've never done it
previously, even though it means I'm missing out on winning
The Ultimate Universe Surf Championships which I've trained
my whole damn life for – but I don't need a stupid trophy; you'
the only girl for me! With no subtlety at all the whole restaurant
are gawking, flabbergasted at us, like we are a flaming meteorit
blasting towards earth. The chef has put down his tools, a white
wine mother tuts, and an old man has placed a strategic cushior
on his lap. Ignoring their meals, they feast on us. They're acting
like they've paid good money to see this kiss. I kiss you harder –
not because I want them to watch, but because the plot says we'
kiss whether they do or not. Let our kisses have kisses! Your tongu
is my dinner and the night is young. Give them popcorn and let then
watch. Let them all watch.

What we did in the car park of Yeats's grave

I am still of opinion that only two topics can be of the least interest to a serious and studious mood – sex and the dead.

WB Yeats

In our camper van, hidden from tourists caked in sunscreen
snapping cameras at lichen-covered gravestones
I meet you where you are

The half-eaten curl their toes, their withered noses
press into the ceilings of their wooden boxes
The dead are jealous

Oh, to be alive and wet, naked on a bunch of pillows!
To have your thrumming tongue inside me. To have
a bluebottle watching us from the sticky olive oil bottle

Oh, to eat your body like white bread! My open legs
an altar you bend to. You are glass I stain
As lough, you leak; I absorb what I can

We will never merge completely
but this is pretty close. I have been trusted
with something holy here

When we are done, I push you out of me
onto a piece of kitchen roll – it's not very romantic
but it is true

You take it from me, fold it gently like origami
then leave, letting the sweaty summer
outside spill in

You take our love to the shimmering, overflowing bin
add it to the fag ends, discarded tickets, licked
lolly sticks and banana skins rotting in the sun

Through the van door, I watch two elderly women
on a picnic bench peacefully eating
egg mayo sandwiches, not saying a word

and maybe it's a post-sex glow, or the heat
or the way one woman lovingly wipes mayonnaise
from her friend's double chin, but God

I feel lucky, lucky to be fucking
under bare Ben Bulben's head
lucky to be so alive, so close to death

Our other lives

In one we are stones in the North Sea, rocking gently until eventually one of us is taken home in a sandal.

In one we are two leaves on a fern, under an old sycamore tree with a rope swing that occasionally whacks us in the wind.

In one we are brothers that finish each other's sentences and laugh at the speed of our hair loss.

In one we are two strangers who meet in the chip shop after a night out. One of us is sick and shoeless; the other takes them home, covers them in a blanket and makes tea and toast. We never see each other again, but we think of each other often.

In one we are two ticks inhabiting a blade of grass, patiently waiting for our next victim.

In one we are two pieces of *Deinococcus radiodurans* bacteria, valuable for our radiation-resistant makeup, growing together on an international space station in a petri dish with a blue sticker, prodded by astronauts every Wednesday.

In one we are connected by our tailbones, unable to shake each other off.

In one we are two parts of the same mycelium network. We only know darkness and damp. Humans don't know how we communicate. We don't have the time to explain.

In one we share a daughter who climbs up walls and has dirty knees; we are in love, we think.

In one we are lemons on a tree, sun beating on our skin until one of us is picked for lemonade and another drizzled on a freshly caught fish.

And in this life we're not together anymore, for whatever reason I cannot mind, but somehow I know for sure I'll see you in the next and the next and the next, in whatever spiritual form is forced on us, for eternity, for the rest of time.

To the baby

You are the length from my middle finger to my elbow, which is also the length of a size-seven shoe. You are asleep on my chest. I keep freaking out that you have stopped breathing, but every time I check so far, you continue. I can't wait for you to talk. I have so much to tell you and I promise to tell you everything. I will tell you about barnacles, that they are soft inside and only stiffen onto rocks as adults. That if you're quiet when you approach you can pick them up and look inside, but you should always put them back where you found them. I'll tell you that trees in Scotland have been mostly planted. I can talk you through the Kardashian family tree but I'm hoping soon it will be irrelevant. I will tell you that the moon is sometimes here and it's sometimes not, that it controls the tides and our moods. I'll tell you that people all over the world have their dinner at 9pm and outside! And I'm sure you won't believe me. I'll say yes, yes they do. They eat fresh tomatoes, drink wine from jugs and chat over bread baskets at 9pm! I'll tell you about bread baskets that may seem like they are free but they're not. I will tell you that I'm hurting. But the good kind. The kind that is painful but feels right. Maybe you'll ask me how I know and I'm not sure I'll have an answer. I will tell you about cities that I have visited and how their skylines look like outstretched arms ready to catch you. I will tell you about how every window represents a life and how that can make you feel small but I'll tell you that's not always a bad thing. I will tell you that soil is cold and rain is wet and that your mum and dad have taught me what love looks like. And when you're old enough I'll tell you that barnacles have massive penises, one of the biggest of any animal in terms of body-to-penis ratio! Today, you know nothing, just the smell of home, your mum's tits and your dad's breath, but someday you'll know more than us and you'll roll your eyes at how dumb we are. You are the first sun and we will rotate around you until you're a teenager and tell us to fuck off. Then we will no doubt drift like aimless stars in awe of all that you are and the passing of time you represent. I check that you are breathing again and you confirm it with a gurgle. You sound like you have a whole world already inside of you and you're ready to burp it all out.

Cherish it

I prayed for joy
until I realised I already had it
It was slower than I had imagined
Moved like syrup off a spoon
and caught me off guard –
on a walk, washing the dishes
a violin sailing through
a tinny speaker on my phone

I prayed for power
until realised I did not want it
Not the blue suit kind anyway
I know it would change me
into someone I would avoid
at a speed dating event or
in a queue at the bank

I prayed for love
until I remembered what
bell hooks said –
Love is action, so I open
the window to let the wasp out
I listen carefully when someone tells me
their name, I look to the dogs
because they are love experts
and they tell me
in their grumpy, gritty voices
Love is effort, a slog
Love is work, baby
and it's more
than a 9-5

I prayed for forgiveness
until I remembered we are all born to sin
How else would we learn
our unbearable lessons?
Aren't we all just bathing in them?
Even the bald monk raking leaves
the toddler waving at the train
Even they don't get it right every time
I thank everything I've done wrong
and I will do better

I prayed for solitude
until I remembered I was already alone
That no one will ever truly know me
not a child, not a reader, not a lover
that I keep for eternity
Even if my bones
one day wash upon the shore
of a different land
and scientists in the lab
prod and poke and
dip me in dye
make a computerised
image of what they think
I looked like
they will not know me
they will not know
what made me cum
what face came to me
in the black windows
what it felt like for me
to eat a mango
over the sink
in the middle of summer
juice dripping down my chin

I prayed for direction
until I realised I am on a one-way system
        – through –
through the bog with its fairies and moss
Its prehistoric wood buried
under layers of muck, ice
the faded Coke can glinting
from the heather. Through
the awkward silences. Through
the death of our parents. Through
the intimacy of our friendships. Through
the sweat and the stains. Through
Monday mornings. Through
dumping and being dumped. Through
having to try, again and again
and that's what hurts
like a nail to the foot

I prayed on my knees
I prayed and prayed
and prayed
until the fabrics of this world
and the others thinned
and I heard a voice say
cherish it

Acknowledgements

Thank you to Colin Bramwell and Janette Ayachi; without your continuous love and confidence I would have quit a long time ago.

Thank you to my mentor Kim Addonizio; she has pulled me forward, and reined me in. Thank you for teaching me how to find doors in my poems and how to open them.

Thank you to my wonderful mum Leonora; this is not easy for us, but I am so grateful that you've never asked me to stop.

Thank you to my dad Rex. Both my parents are/were exceptional storytellers.

Thank you to The Girls – Chrissy, Court, Fems, Hazy, Heady, Kizo, Liv, Maz, Monique, Rosie, Sia and the rest of my pals (especially Joe and Ruairi). Thank you for all the cackling and giving me plenty of material.

Thank you to Aimee and Ashleigh, who housed me on the final stretch of this book.

Thank you to my family – my aunties and cousins, especially Grace, Sadie, Leslie, Kerry and Larah.

Thank you to all my mum's friends, our chosen family.

Thank you to Jack and the McCuddens, who picked pride over embarrassment every time.

Thank you to my CPP family; you taught me everything I know and love about making.

Thank you to Rachelle Atalla, Hannah Kelso, Iona Lee and the early morning writers' group who make this writing life feel less lonely.

Thank you to Claire Askew, who mentored me through the beginning of this journey.

Thank you to Charlotte and Tom at the Lyth Theatre – I had the most magical time.

Thanks to Big Gina; we got a lot of writing done, didn't we?

Thank you to Bridget, Clive and Harriet at Burning Eye – it has been a pleasure. Thanks for the trust.

Thank you to Creative Scotland for funding the development stage of this book.

Thank you to all the organisations, events, venues, charities, teachers and librarians I've worked with over the years. There's too many to name, but you know who you are.

Thank you to all the people that I teach and write with – writing with you is my best fun and greatest honour.

Thank you to all of you reading this book or coming to the shows – you are the only reason that any of this makes any sense.

Finally, thank you to my dyslexia, a magical beast that leads me into strange woods. I'm sorry it's taken me this long to realise what a legend you are. Thank you, thank you, thank you.

Credits

'Good with our hands' was first published in Gutter magazine and then in Scottish Poetry Library's online anthology *Best Scottish Poems of 2020*.

'Being Scottish' was a commission by Edinburgh International Book Festival for Literature Live Around the World.

A version of 'Pompeii' was first published in Neu! Reekie!'s #*UntitledThree*.

Versions of 'The morning after' and 'Times like these (2020)' were first published in The Alchemy Experiment's magazine *Love in the Time of Covid*.

The poem 'What Do Women Want?' was inspired by Kim Addonizio's 'What Do Women Want?'.

'Maman' is inspired by a series of sculptures called *Maman* by Louise Bourgeois.

A version of 'Questions I have for birds' was first published in Edwin Morgan's *Centenary Collection* published by Speculative Books.

'Elizabeth and her house' was a commission from Feral Art's audio series *My Own Private Audio*.

'Dear John Berger' was inspired by BBC documentary series/ book *Ways of Seeing*.

The line 'under bare Ben Bulben's head' from 'What we did in the car park of Yeats's grave' is a line from W.B.Yeats's poem 'Under Ben Bulben'.

'Our other lives' was first published by SWSN Zine Vol. 2.

Lightning Source UK Ltd.
Milton Keynes UK
UKHW040620261022
411112UK00003B/39